Scraps
Remnants of the Girl I Left Behind

Scraps

There's a certain art to scrap metal
The idea of a device
Or a person
Being gutted, torn apart,
With only the useful pieces allowed to remain

These pieces are given a value and then
Constructed by someone else into what
They need; what they want

And the metal has no choice but
To become a twisted and demented version
Of its former glory

I have been torn apart and
Left for scraps
Too many times to count

Every time I am rebuilt
I am nothing more than a shell
Nothing more than a
Monstrosity
A heap of scraps sewn together

Rusted and ruined
And so far from my
Intended purpose

I didn't intend to
Live like this
I don't know if I could call this
Living, at all

Table of Contents

Conversations With Sydney (I)

i call her on the telephone and
she picks up
i tell her something's wrong;
she asks me   *what happened?*

and all do is cry into the phone
and she says   *take deep breaths*

and my tears are gone
but i still can't speak

so i hang up

she texts me right after
she wants to know   *what's wrong*
but i can't tell her   *what's wrong*

i have never been so afraid
of being vulnerable

i say nevermind
she doesn't buy it
she asks again   *what's wrong*
                                  what's wrong
                                  what's wrong
and i ask myself   *what's wrong*

i tell her she has nothing to worry about
she tells me she's here for me
somehow, that makes me feel
a little worse

recently, i started
talking to elizabeth
i call her on the telephone and
she picks up

i tell her a problem
and she helps in the way
no one can usually help

i do not
talk to
sydney
i can not
talk to
sydney
i do not
dare

there is this aching part of me
that is petrified she will
finally see how weak i am

because
what if i
tell her that
sometimes i
contemplate the
world without me

not in a bad way
but i let my thoughts drift
and somehow i keep ending up there

i know she will not be cruel
i know she cares about me

but i am afraid

i do not
talk to
sydney

somehow, that makes me feel
a little worse

The Fall Of The Friend Or Foe

I didn't want to hurt you
I know that I did
Somehow
I know that something went wrong

I don't know what happened
I only remember flashes
I only remember the pain

I don't remember what you said
Only that I came home and spent hours crying
I don't remember what caused it
I don't remember why you decided I wasn't
Good enough
I don't know if I ever knew

I've asked you since it all happened
It's been two years and I still can't
Wrap my head around it
But you don't remember
I don't know why I expected
Anything else

I don't quite know when we stopped being friends
I don't quite know when we fixed things
Fixed things in a temporary sort of way
Put a band-aid on a bullet wound
I shoved the feelings of hurt down
Deep into my chest

Elizabeth,
I care about you
I don't know what happened
When we turned from friend to foe

When you stopped being my confidant,
My closest friend,
And started being my nightmare

I tried so hard to navigate the minefield that was the
Crumbling remains of our friendship
I tried so hard to get us both out
Unscathed

But you were determined to be
The only victor

You'd always been competitive
I didn't realize that existing was an extreme sport

In movies, they paint bullies as these powerful people
Who you are taught to be afraid of
But I was never afraid of you

I suppose that was the problem

Conversations With Sydney (II)

elizabeth doesn't talk to me
when she does, it's pointless words
a need to fill the silence that strangles us

she has moved on in the way that
i can not move on

sydney has moved on too
not to say that she does not care,
but we are distant

she asks me   *what's wrong*
but the words are all wrong
she is not
the same girl that i knew
it is my fault
i know

i corroded our friendship,
rusted it in the way
oxygen takes to metal
the pieces are still there
but everything has changed

yet still
she calls me on the telephone
and i pick up

and it is weird and uncomfortable
and silent more often than not
we are like perfect strangers
connected only by people we used to be

sometimes i find myself trying to
make my relationship with sydney
like my relationship with elizabeth
but my relationship with sydney is
not like my relationship with elizabeth

it isn't until weeks after i have
finally accepted that
elizabeth and i are no longer friends
that i notice the change
when i call her,
choking on silent sobs
saying nothing and
terrified and so close to
hanging up the phone
but clutching it like a lifeline
sydney asks me   *what's wrong*

elizabeth
never did that

Therapy Session With God

I'm sorry that this isn't our usual time
To be honest,
I'm don't know if we have a usual time
I don't know if I want one

But right now,
I suppose I need you
Need you in a weird and arbitrary way
Need you because I need answers

I suppose because I am lost
Confused

I suppose it is as if I am running out of air
Running like a tank on empty
Running until there is nothing left

I've been wondering if it is possible for You to
Make mistakes
People say everything happens for a reason
And I am not doubting that
But I wonder

Satan Walks Into A Bar

Satan walks into a bar
And you remind yourself that
You are an angel
Pure and unadulterated
White feathers of perfection

You are an angel
In a heaven of your own design

You are
Just like everyone else

Satan walks into a bar
Sits next to you
Flashes a smile
And you are reminded that
You and satan
Are nothing alike
But yet
You are alike

Satan walks into a bar
Tells you that you
Look so good
In that dress
That you have the
Nicest smile
She's ever seen
That you are the
Nicest girl she'll ever meet
That you
Are the best friend
She'd ever had

Satan walks out of the Bar
Reminds you
Not to be a stranger
Reminds you
Not to be a stranger
Reminds you
Everything is okay

Satan walks into a bar
Buys you a drink
Waits for your smile
Satan calls you later
That night

She's the one
Who hangs up

Satan walks into a bar and
You sit with all the
Other angels
All the other girls who
Are just like you

Satan walks into a bar
But she starts talking to
All the other angels
And you wonder what happened to
You having the nicest smile

Satan walks into a bar
And she tells someone else
That they have the
Nicest smile
She's ever seen
That they are the
Nicest girl she'll ever meet
That they
Are the best friend
She's ever had

Satan walks into a bar
And doesn't even say
Hi to you

Satan walks out of the bar
And you want to remind her
Not to be a stranger
Not to be a stranger
And this girl
Is a stranger
Reminds you
Everything isn't okay

You are an angel
In a heaven of your own perfection
But this heaven is
Starting to look
More like hell
And this world is
Starting to look
More like hell

Satan walks into a bar
Or
An angel walks into a bar
Or
She walks into a bar
And she leaves you there

The Definition Of Normalcy

I've stopped taking my medication
Figured I shouldn't need to
Swallow 15 pills to feel
Normal and I feel my head start to hurt
Until I go back on

And it rings
Like a pounding in my ears
Like I'm everyone's favorite freak show

Like there's
Nothing I could do to
Ever feel normal

Some days
There is nothing I want more than
To not be different
Than to be perfectly normal
than to look in the mirror and see a girl
Who looks like every other person is this room

Because "normal" people
Don't sit and contemplate how
Lonely they feel all the fucking time

Normal people don't
Contemplate their existence
Every other day

And I've seen
The stares as I walk down the halls
And the looks
And my mind starts to race
Because my shirt and my shoes feel
Out of place
And i feel out of place
And what am I doing here?

My mother will tell me
It's all in my head
It's me psyching myself out of just
Living my own damn life

But how can I live this way
When I know that I'm
Nothing compared to
Whoever is gonna walk down that
Hallway next

And I look in the mirror and I see
Everything that is wrong with this world

And I try to write a poem
That's not about my
Lack of self-esteem but

But all that comes out is a
Mumbled piece of garbage
That looks just like me

I stopped taking my medication
Figured I shouldn't need
15 or 20 pills to make me feel like
Every other person on this goddamn planet

Like maybe
If I suffer enough
I'll finally
Be normal

Because She's Real

I've been doing this thing recently
Where I've been trying not to focus too much on
Black and white
And look more at the
Grey areas because
Everything's
A grey area and
I've invented this version of her
In my head
That doesn't match up to the one in front of me
Because she's right in front of me
Because she's real

And she's not a
Disney villain
Or Regina George from Mean Girls

She's the girl I've known since middle school
The girl I was scared to lose
The girl I finally let go of
But just keep crawling back to

She's not
Cruella de Vil
Or Darth Vader
She's the girl I called every night in eighth grade
She's the girl who always had my back
She's the girl who turned her back on me

And a part of me wonders if she ever cared about me
In the way I cared about her
The way you do when someone is your
Best friend
And sometimes I wonder
If that feeling was ever mutual

And I've been Imagining my life
And playing it out
Over and over again
Imagining a world where she was
The hero and I, her sidekick
But instead it's different

Instead she is the
Hero and I am The villain
Ruining her perfect world
Needing to be eradicated

I keep making
Storybook analogies
But the thing about storybooks is
They're divided
So easily

Good and bad
Black and white
Right and wrong

I want to believe I am the good guy
But if I was the hero
Why couldn't I do anything to defend myself?
If I was the hero
Why did I just run?
And if it makes more sense that I am
The villain
In this fairytale
Does that make me a bad person?
If I fell to pieces from her wrath
And haven't quite been whole since

I'm just not quite sure where I stand
And if, after everything
I should be the one to say
I'm sorry

Caution Sign

I was in middle school
I was young and naive
And she was sweet
She was captivating

I didn't think
She would like me at first
I was nervous but
She was sweet
Sweet like butterscotch candies
That get stuck in your braces
For hours on end
She's the kind of sweet that rots your teeth
And leaves you breathless
And you keep coming back
Because you just can't see
The damage

But I was young
I hadn't ever dealt with girls like her before
And I wanted to connect with someone
I was lonely and desperate for a friend
And I try to tell myself
That's why I went to her
And not because I wanted to
I don't want to think that I wanted to
But I wanted to

I ignored the caution sign
And slipped on tiles wet with forgotten tears
I ignored the caution sign
And was met with the
Demolition zone of our friendship
I ignored the caution sign
And walked into the fire

Vibrant

I am a white canvas
Covered in white colored pencil
Boring and bland
And waiting for colors

And I see her
And she's vibrant
Blues and purples and greens
She is vibrant and I am jealous
She is vibrant and
I am ashamed

I am a splotchy canvas
Covered in her colors
Trying to absorb the best parts of her
Because I'd rather be vibrant than
Boring and bland and
I'd rather be a phony than something
No one wants around

Because why display a mistake
A blank canvas
When you have a masterpiece

But I am nothing but a knock-off
Nothing but a sorry replacement
And my colors are dull
I am not vibrant
I am ashamed

I am a ruined canvas
Covered in so many colors that
Anything once beautiful is
Muddy and fake and dirty

I am ripped
Torn to shreds and pretending I
Can stitch myself back together

I am not vibrant
I am not whole
I am ashamed

I am sick
Sick of trying to be better than what I am
Sick of trying to be a masterpiece when
I am only scribbles
Only a painting done by a child
Or a blind woman
Or someone who doesn't know
What art is

I am sick of
Trying to be
Vibrant

Because maybe I am not vibrant
Maybe my colors are muted and
Maybe my mind and heart are dull

Maybe I am
Not the masterpiece I wish to be
But at least I am something

And maybe one day
That will be enough
Maybe one day I'll stop being
Ashamed

Lost Things

I'll close my eyes and I'll try to
Picture it
Picture you
But everything just turns out fuzzy

Like how you cut your hair and
All of my picture of us are from before

And someday,
I'll look at these photos and say
"This is enough" but
Today is not that day

The mirror in my bedroom reflects how
I still have your book
And your scrunchie
And your letters

"Open when
You miss me"
I open it every day

And it's hard
When every pair of converse I own seems like a
Knock-off version of you

Like maybe, if I close my eyes hard enough,
The last three months will disappear

And I know I'm being ridiculous, but
I miss our 12 am conversations
And your bubbly laughter

You still laugh but
You don't laugh with me

And I have that but
It's not enough
It's never enough

And I'm not going to
Get back to Sunday morning
Teasing you about your shoe size or
Pillow fights in the moonlight of daybreak

And one day
I'll look at these shoes and see
Only these shoes but
Today is not that day

Because every time
I close my eyes
I hear echoes and see your face
And your smile
And your eyes

And one day
That'll be enough

But it's not like
We don't talk

And I know
She misses me

I didn't miss her so much until
She didn't miss me anymore

And one day
I'll look at your smile,
And I'll know
I'm not the cause

And one day,
That will be enough

Happy Birthday

I want to pretend I don't
Still care about you

I want to pretend
Your birthday isn't saved in my phone or
Pretend I miss talking effortlessly with you

I got a notification this morning
Saying that it was your birthday,
But the calendar confirmed what I already knew

On Instagram that day
I see photos of
You and your new
Friends (who are
Still just your old friends
But without me in the picture)
And I try to stamp out the
Flames of jealousy and longing
And remind myself that
I'm not friends with you anymore
Because you didn't want me
Because you kicked me out

But there are days when my
Reasons for staying away
Are driven out by the reminder of
How happy I was
How happy I could have been
If I was still there

And I start going
Down memory lane

I remember
Seventh grade
Sitting next to you in civics and
Eighth grade
Sharing secrets over the phone

I remember
Eighth grade,
And looking back I wonder how
I didn't see this coming

I remember how
I got you a
Tiara for your
Fourteenth birthday, but
That was the same year
You decided
I wasn't good enough
For you

It's hard for me to come to terms with
The fact that I miss you
Because you were so shitty to me
That I shouldn't miss you
But I don't know how I could not

I don't know how to deal with the fact that
Every time I think of you,
I feel like I lost something

I don't know how to feel about the fact
That I wish I was there

I wish I hadn't let you down
And ruined our friendship
And I don't know what I did
But I'm sorry

Happy Birthday,
Elizabeth
I hope it was fun

An Apology Letter To My Ex-Girlfriend

I'm sorry for wasting your time
There were plenty of other people
You could have given those months to, but i took them
And like everything I take,
I ruined them

I'm sorry for keeping photos of you
And letters you wrote me
And birthday cards
I'm sorry
But I just don't know what to do with them
And there's a part of me
That doesn't want to throw them away

It never felt like a long relationship
Until I realized that everything reminds me of you
Reminds me of the friendship I ruined
And can never get back

I'm sorry for lying to you
I've tried to convince myself that
I wasn't lying at the time
But the idea is hard to come to terms with

I'm sorry for saying yes
I'm sorry for taking you to school dances
And worrying you
And letting you give me your heart
I'm sorry for not returning the favor
I'm sorry I had nothing to give

I'm sorry for the way I ended things
I'm sorry that I couldn't stay
And that I felt like I needed to stay
and I'm sorry
For hurting you

If there is anyone who didn't deserve that
It's you

And I don't know why I'm writing a letter
That you'll never read
An apology left better unsaid
You've moved on and
I've moved on but
I can't live with the idea
Of you not knowing that I'm sorry

I'm sorry for
Feeling nothing

I feel like a
Broken record by now
And sometimes
Broken is the best word to describe me
I'm sorry for not
Loving you
The way you wanted me to

I'm sorry
I couldn't be what you deserve

Drowning

The first time I watched the movie Jaws,
I wasn't afraid
For some reason,
The shark attacks didn't scare me

I was not scared
Until I watched the second movie
And I got to the scene with the
Kids on the inflatable boat

These kids, all alone, could
Easily die out here
And no one would know

You remind me of these kids
Helpless
Shoved into the water
Before you know how to swim
And you claim you're fine
A little water never hurt anybody

Suddenly she comes near you
Teeth bared
Looking to attack
But you pretend her fangs are a smile
She is capable of cutting you in half
But you tell yourself
She won't

She may be a predator
But she likes you
She may be hunting
But she's keeping you safe

You don't want to be afraid
Most days you are not
But some days,
You are

She keeps you within her grasp
Trapped in a circle of sharks
And you can't move without becoming the prey
But you pretend the sharks are harmless
Pretend you're not afraid

You see the blood in the water
You pretend it isn't your own
Pretend you're not in pain
And you know what she is capable of
You know how quickly she could turn on you
And what she could do if she did

But you tell yourself
She won't

She may be a shark
But she is smiling

And I'm trying so hard
To save you from yourself
But I can't pull you ashore
Or drag you away and onto the sandy beaches where
You'll finally be safe
I can't keep you afloat
If you don't even know
You're drowning

I don't know how to save you
From this ocean
That you're unwilling to swim out of
I can't throw you a life preserver
If you're unwilling to take it

But we are more alike
Than I care to admit

And if I can not save you,
Because I am too busy drowning as well
If I am surrounded by my own
Circle of sharks closing in
Drawing blood

I refuse to take the life preserver thrown to me
Maybe I can see why you do, too

So I sit here
And watch you float farther and farther out to sea
Your lungs filling with the salty water
And as you slowly slip beneath the waves

I can do
Nothing
But watch

Numb

she reminds me
of winter
all snow
and ice
and cold stone heart

she reminds me
of sunlight

she is brutal
solid stone or concrete
the harsh white of the hospital

she is a whirlwind
like pricking your finger on a spinning wheel
you feel high and vulnerable all at the same time
and then
you feel nothing

i wish i could say i am still angry
or sad
i wish i could say i feel anything

but wallowing in sorrow has gotten me nowhere
living in rage has left me scarred from the inferno of my
own hellfire

it is better,
i suppose,
to be numb

I Want You To Care About Me

I want you to care about me
You tell me I'm overthinking it
Say that you do
I know you do
But I want you to care the way I do

I hate the fact that
You're the most important thing in my life

Hate how even when I step away from you
I still think about you over and over

I hate that I'm so easily let down

I hate that I let you become so important to me
So quickly

I let you mean so much to me
And I don't know how to feel
When you don't feel the same

And I know it's not your fault
That I get attached too quickly
That I feel broken when you care about other people
When I remember
You don't feel the same way about me
As I feel about you

There are days
When I don't know how to define love
I don't understand the romantic kind but
I understand this

I want to be around you all the time
Seeing you makes my smile wider and my heart happier

Seeing you makes everything better
And sometimes it makes everything worse
Because I remember that
I love you with every fiber of being

And to you,
I am nothing.
To you,
I am replaceable.
To you,
I am clingy
And annoying
And the girl who never seems to want to leave your side

I want you to care about me
But more than anything,
I want you to love me

My Mother Tells Me She Is Afraid

My mother tells me she is afraid
Some days, I don't know if she is afraid of me or for me
I know that she is consumed by this worry
This ever-present fear
I know she is scared
I can almost understand why

Except for some days, when I don't
Some days, when I don't understand
How she could ever be
More afraid than I am
Like every single part of me isn't screaming with anger
Teeming with fear

I have nearly given up
Trying to make molehills out of mountains
Nearly given up trying to pretend
This is less serious and terrifying than it really is
Nearly given up trying not to be afraid

I am too scared to pretend I'm not afraid
My mother is too
She reminds me of how priceless I am
Sobbing in the dead of night and
Wiping her eyes before she worries me
She does not want to worry me
She doesn't want me to see
How scared she is
She doesn't want me to worry about her

But it is impossible not to worry
She is so scared she will lose me
She makes me scared, too

In Which She Shatters

In which the girl attempts to
Not fall apart

In which she runs from her problems,
Chipping off pieces of her happiness
Until little remains

In which the girl is sad
And she used to think it was normal but
She knows it is not
Normal but
She doesn't want help
She doesn't need help

In which she knows, in the back of her mind
She needs help

In which she stops taking her medication
Doesn't know if it's helping
Decides she's done
Feeling like a fuck up who needs correcting

In which she watches herself break
And doesn't do anything

In which the girl needs
Connection
Comfort
Companionship

In which the girl
Walks away

In which she knows
She's unhealthy
But she doesn't know how to stop
And she wonders if she wants to

In which she makes suicide jokes
And wonders if she's joking

In which the idea of resting in peace
Sounds really fucking good

In which she
Shatters

In which the girl attempts to put herself back together
But can't recognize
Any of the pieces

An Ode To The Nights I Think About Overdosing

I look to Tylenol, first
Wonder if it is strong enough to kill me
I think of the effects of an overdose
Think of the slow and painful death
And the most common side effect:
Total organ failure

I think about how
I am not sure I want to die
Think about the things I have left to do
And wonder about the pain I would feel if I failed

If I tried to kill myself
And I didn't succeed
If I was left with
Fucked up organs and
Another reason for my
Parents to hate me

I hesitate to call myself suicidal because
I know this is more like ideation
I don't have any intention to
Actually end my life,
I know I wouldn't be able to it's just
The thought is nice,
Sometimes

I don't plan to commit suicide
I just think about it
Often
More than I should
More than is healthy

I take "are you suicidal?" quizzes I find online
Hoping the answer will tell me something I want to hear,
Tell me I'm normal

I think there is something to be said
For the fact that I am taking these quizzes
In the first place
People who are not suicidal
Do not waste time wondering if they are

I tell my Mother about my suicidal ideation and
She is so scared
She threatens to have me institutionalized
Like her fear will keep my demons away

She accuses me of threatening her with suicide
As if I'm doing this just to spite her
Because these feelings can not otherwise be valid

I think of the slow and painful death
And know I am too scared to ever go through with it
Too scared of the pain and
Too scared to leave everyone behind

But sometimes I wonder if
Dying is what it would take for them
To care about me enough to want me to stay

On nights like these
I look at the bottle of Tylenol
And wonder if a painful death is
Something I deserve, after all

Temporary Relapse

I hate being sick in a way unlike
Anything I've ever hated before
I love being sick, too

That's what makes recovery so difficult
That's what makes me so scared

Teetering on the edge of a relapse
So close to falling
But barely hanging on

I do not miss being sick
But I miss the ache of depression
seeping into my bones
I miss the manic magic
All focus and fire and fuel
I miss feeling whole
You forget that this sickness is a part of you
You don't know who you are without this disease

This is not quite relapse
But some days it feels close enough

It is not healthy
But it is safe

Fearless

I am terrified to talk to you
Looking at you reminds me of
Everything you've done wrong and
Everything I've done wrong and
The gap that keeps widening
Between us

I am afraid of losing you
But I am also afraid of reconnecting

I'm afraid of getting attached
Like I did before
I'm afraid of being hurt again

Really,
I am afraid to trust anyone
I am afraid to trust you

And I wonder how foolish that sounds
Because I know how deeply
I wish I could trust you

I am debilitated by this fear
And I hate that I am not over it by now
I hate that it has been two years and
I can barely look at you without
Thinking of how awful you made me feel

I wish I could have courage
I wish I could be brave and just talk to you
Without feeling like a failure

But I am so
Afraid of being hurt
And I hate that I'm not over it
I don't know how I could be

You asked me what I call courage
The first thing out of my mouth
Is "fear"

A Poem About Healing

This is not a poem
About Elizabeth

This is a poem
About healing

This is a poem
About me

I want to trust her
I want to be warm and welcoming
And I want things
To go back to before

But I can not
Go back to before

I can not
Pretend that the worst year of my life
Didn't happen

I do not hate her
I don't think I ever could but
I hate what she did
I hate feeling like a broken doll
Like a wind-up toy
Missing a crank

I hate the days
When I feel like I'm not good enough
Because why else would
You have done it?

You do not discard a perfectly good doll
You return the ones with
Broken legs and chipped paint

You return the ones that
Break your friend's heart
The ones that
Are clingy and mean and dirty
You return the friends that are
Broken beyond repair

I want to learn how to sew,
If anything, so I can fix myself
The way I'd be able to
Fix a blanket or clothes with holes in them
If I could stitch myself back together
Maybe I could finally heal

I know
It doesn't work like that

But I am
Optimistic

My parents think I'm stupid for trusting you
They're probably right

After all,
How can I know
You don't look at me
And still see broken pieces

Or worse:
How do I know you
Won't step on the parts

That you won't take one look at this
Shattered mess
Masquerading as a girl and decide that
I am worthless
That I am not worthy of air
Or your time

How do I know
You won't break me

How can I trust you
After everything that's happened

I don't know why
I am drawn to you like
A moth to a flame, like
I was all those years ago

But if you
Try to break me again
This time
I will not shatter

Glass Shards

The floor is littered with glass shards
Sharp and pointy
Remnants of the girl who used to live here
Live in my body; in my life
Some days, I am glad she is
Shattered and ruined on my floor
And not living and breathing
In front of me

Once I tried to throw away the pieces, but
This trash bag felt too much like a body bag
And I refused to let you
Leave like that

I started wearing shoes in the house
Big and bulky and thick;
Enough to dull the blade of any piece I step on

I'd rather lock my feet up than pick up the pieces
I'm afraid the sharp edge of this girl on the floor
Will cut me
I can not sweep this under the rug
And yet… I can not live with the remains

An Apology Letter To Myself

I'm sorry for wasting your time
You spent years chasing girls who wanted
Nothing to do with you
Spent years shoving dark thoughts down your throat

I'm sorry for keeping old poems
Snapshots of when I was happy
And sad
I'm sorry that this book is a
Collage of all the reasons I used to hate myself
But it is a joy to be able to say I
Use to

I'm sorry
For hurting you

I'm sorry
For convincing you to hate every
Imperfection in your skin
In your brain
I'm sorry I convinced you that
You were worthless

But you are not worthless
You are not an amalgamation of
Everything you've ever done wrong
You are beautiful
In your weird, stupid sort of way

I'm sorry for lying to you
For telling you these things
I'm sorry for believing them

I'm sorry
I can't be what you deserve
But I'm trying

An Apology Letter To You

I'm sorry if this is not the poetry book
You were expecting
I'm sorry that my life is not the
Happy ending
You were looking for

I am sorry I could not sugarcoat
The darkness in my life
Sorry it is all raw
And bruised hearts,
Scraped knees,
Bloody knuckles

This is the body of a girl
Who has survived herself

This is the body of girl
Who is not ready to give up

So I'm sorry if this book is not
The happy ending you've been expecting
But my life is not
Happily ever after
But it is getting there

Acknowledgements

For my parents, who always support me in everything I do. Thank you for being my anchor in the roaring sea of my trauma.

For my brother, Scott, who always knows what to say. Thank you for never having doubt in me.

For my Grandmother, who always encouraged me to write. Thank you for building me into the woman I am today.

For Isabella, the best friend and sister I never knew I needed. Thank you for always listening, even when you had nothing to say.

For Kayla, my rock. Thank you for being splices of normalcy in the black hole of my life. Thank you for being a constant in my life since freshman year.

For Allison, who keeps me going. Thank you for always being there, even since we were kids. You have faced your own demons the same way I have, but when we stand together, the monsters don't seem half as bad.

For Sophie, who makes my life a better place to live. Thank you for reminding me that the world is full of joy, even in the sad times. The world would be dull without your light.

For Alison, my cover artist, and more importantly, my friend. Thank you for engaging me in the deep and awkward conversations, the ones full of opinions we are too scared to speak.

For Sydney, who reminds me that friendships only die when you let them.

For Elizabeth, my best friend for years. Thank you for reminding me what it is to feel. Thank you for mending things. I'm proud of us and how much we've grown.

For my younger self, I'm so proud of you. Thank you for never backing down from a challenge. Thank you for continuing on, even when things got difficult. I am so proud of you.

Author Bio

Emma Wasserman is a poet, actress, and crazy cat lady. A proud member of Gen Z, she strongly believes in the power of the youth. She has two complete works, a poetry collection entitled "Scraps: Remnants of the Girl I Left Behind" and a play entitled "Dead Ball." She currently resides in Davie, Florida, with her parents and her two cats, Sterling and Calliope.

Made in the USA
Columbia, SC
22 December 2020